THE
POWER OF 2:

WORK+DESIRE=SUCCESS

WORKBOOK *for couples*

How To Succeed in
Business and in Marriage

ERIC KIRK

Jai Publishing House Incorporated
1230 Peachtree Street NE | 19th Floor Atlanta, Georgia 30309
www.jaipublishing.com

Scripture taken from the New King James Version®. Copyright © 1982 by Thomas Nelson. Used by permission. All rights reserved.

The Publisher is not responsible for websites (or their content) that are not owned by the publisher.
The views expressed in this publication are those of the author and do not necessarily reflect the official policy or position of any other agency, organization, employer or company associated with the publisher.

Printed in the United States of America
ISBN-13: 9781736661352

☛DISCLAIMER☚
All products and services by the author are for educational and informational purposes only. Your level of success in attaining any stated ideas or strategies in the programs or on the author's websites is dependent upon several factors including your health, skill, knowledge, ability, dedication, goals, relationships, love of other humans, and financial situation, to name a few.

As stipulated by law, the author makes no guarantees that you will achieve any specific results from the information presented in this book, programs or services and offer no licensed or professional medical, legal, therapeutic, tax, or financial advice in this book. The information contained herein cannot replace or substitute for the services of trained professionals in any field, including, but not limited to, medical, psychological, financial, or legal matters.

Revelations

#1

Man Was Not Meant To Be Alone

#2

Accountability

#3

Protection

#4

Motivation

#5

Correction

#6

Agreement

#7

Keep the Fire Burning

#8

Small Is the New Big With God

CONTENTS

PART 1

MIND, BODY & SOUL

Creating and managing emotional, mental and physical health is vital to the success of a relationship. This section will address matters of the heart.

PART 2

BUILD YOUR BUSINESS

A comprehensive step–by–step guide to building a business together, in the Power of 2, with accountability measures for success.

PART 3

RESOURCES

Tools, tips, tricks, templates, and more to get started on your business immediately.

THE POWER OF 2 *the agreement*

Attach, glue, staple, draw a picture of a current photograph of each partner.
Underneath the picture, write a statement of commitment to this workbook and this
process. You may need to refer back to it later! This is your "Why".

_____

_____

_____

_____

_____

_____

_____

ABOUT THIS WORKBOOK

"The Power of 2: Work+Desire=Success" is an interactive workbook experience designed to create successful marriages and careers.

This workbook asks questions, makes observations, teaches how to stop issues before they start, and challenges partners to improve their personal strengths.

Included in this workbook are practical assignments that take place outside the pages of this book with tips, tools and resources to aid in the #Powerof2x journey.

Grab your bibles, partner, Faith, Reason, Will, Werk and Desire, and let's go!

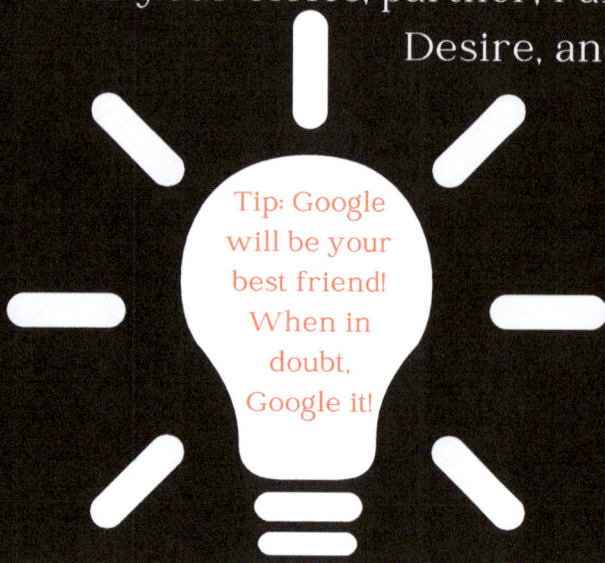

Tip: Google will be your best friend! When in doubt, Google it!

-Eric Kirk

How to Use

THIS WORKBOOK #POWEROF2X

SET YOUR INTENTIONS

Set your goals FIRST! Be clear on what each of you expect from the other. Set your rules, agree, sign, and get to work! #Powerof2x

CHOOSE A FOCUS

The best way to eat an elephant is one bite at a time!

⊙ Only focus on one section of this workbook at a time – until both parties agree to move to the next section. #Powerof2x

BLOCK TIME

Set aside a dedicated time to work through your #Powerof2x activities

OUR TIMETABLE

Monday

Tuesday

Wednesday

Thursday

Friday

WHAT YOU WILL NEED...

- writing tool
- magazines, newspapers
- personal journal
- a partner
- an open mind
- internet (research)

part one

THE POWER OF 2

MIND, BODY, & SOUL

Date: _____   Partners: _____

Goals Planner
FOR THE MARRIAGE

Our Goals	Motivations

Actions to Take	Deadline
☐ _____	_____
☐ _____	_____
☐ _____	_____
☐ _____	_____
☐ _____	_____
☐ _____	_____

Important Dates

January
- ○ _____
- ○ _____
- ○ _____

February
- ○ _____
- ○ _____
- ○ _____

March
- ○ _____
- ○ _____
- ○ _____

April
- ○ _____
- ○ _____
- ○ _____

May
- ○ _____
- ○ _____
- ○ _____

June
- ○ _____
- ○ _____
- ○ _____

July
- ○ _____
- ○ _____
- ○ _____

August
- ○ _____
- ○ _____
- ○ _____

September
- ○ _____
- ○ _____
- ○ _____

October
- ○ _____
- ○ _____
- ○ _____

November
- ○ _____
- ○ _____
- ○ _____

December
- ○ _____
- ○ _____
- ○ _____

Note :
_____
_____

Weekly Planner

URGENT
- ○ ....
- ○ ....
- ○ ....

sunday
- ○ ....
- ○ ....
- ○ ....

monday
- ○ ....
- ○ ....
- ○ ....

tuesday
- ○ ....
- ○ ....
- ○ ....

wednesday
- ○ ....
- ○ ....
- ○ ....

thursday
- ○ ....
- ○ ....
- ○ ....

friday
- ○ ....
- ○ ....
- ○ ....

saturday
- ○ ....
- ○ ....
- ○ ....

CREATIVE WORKSHOP

THE

POWER OF 2:

WORK+DESIRE=SUCCESS

Mind

How to care for the mental health of the
business and marital relationship

#THEPOWEROF2X

SELF-CARE 101

Empowering you to create and maintain a self-care plan to strengthen your inner core

Dear #Powerof2x Partners:

Self-care is an important part of our ability to live life to the fullest – meaning we are able to give our 100% to whatever task we are taking on for that moment. If we do not practice self-care, we often find ourselves sluggish, fatigue, aggravated, irritated... and then it can go deeper into poor dieting, lack of sleep, unable to focus on a task... and y'all know what's next, it begins to affect our mental health and even our physical body! And not feeling your best can lead to disagreements and separation.

Self-care is more than just taking care of our physical body, let's be clear. So in this workbook, we will develop self-care routines that could increase our mental, physical and spiritual health.

We put together a list of things you can do to include in your self-care regimen, that's right.. it needs to be a regular routine for the both of you. Put it on your calendar, schedule time for yourself and for one another, be intentional, and be committed to being the best YOU that you can be. #Powerof2x

This list is not, by all means, the end all be all. Pick and choose the ones that work for you, your partner, your family, and your lifestyle. That means you may experience a little trial and error until you find the right fit!

Don't choose anything that will cause anxiety or discomfort, that defeats the whole purpose of self-care!

DEVELOP A SELF CARE REGIMEN BASED ON YOUR FAMILY'S LIFESTYLE

"As important as it is to have a plan for doing work, it is perhaps more important to have a plan for rest, relaxation, self-care, and sleep." -Akiroq Brost

EAT WELL

Cook together!

REFRESH

Take mini breaks throughout the day

REST

A tired mind cannot be rational – take a break

SELFCARE *for couples*

THE ART OF PAYING ATTENTION TO YOU AND YOUR PARTNER NEEDS

FEED YOUR SPIRITUAL SELF

Fellowship, read the Word together

WIND DOWN

Engage in calming activities to decompress after work or school

SOCIAL

Spend quality time with each other (date night!)

KNOW YOURSELF

Do more of what brings you joy in the relationship

SELF CARE

In the boxes, describe and draw practical ways you and your partner can show self-care in your relationship

THE
POWER OF 2:
WORK+DESIRE=SUCCESS

VACATION PLANNER

This section helps you organize future trips, destinations, shopping lists, flight informations, etc.

Travel Bucket List

DESTINATION 1

- [ ]
- [ ]
- [ ]
- [ ]
- [ ]
- [ ]
- [ ]
- [ ]

DESTINATION 2

- [ ]
- [ ]
- [ ]
- [ ]
- [ ]
- [ ]
- [ ]
- [ ]

DESTINATION 3

- [ ]
- [ ]
- [ ]
- [ ]
- [ ]
- [ ]
- [ ]
- [ ]

DESTINATION 4

- [ ]
- [ ]
- [ ]
- [ ]
- [ ]
- [ ]
- [ ]
- [ ]

Travel Planner

Date :

DESTINATION

- [ ]
- [ ]
- [ ]
- [ ]
- [ ]

ADDRESS

REMINDER

PLACE TO EAT

PLACE TO SHOP

BUDGET

FOOD _____

SOUVENIRS _____

DRINKS _____

OTHER _____

Our Notes

Date :

WHILE WE ARE AWAY

TASK	WHO'S RESPONSIBLE

CREATIVE
WORKSHOP

THE

POWER OF 2:

WORK+DESIRE=SUCCESS

Body

How to care for the physical health of the business and marital relationship

#THEPOWEROF2X

Medical Appointment

Date	Description	Doctor	Notes

Allergies, Blood Type, Other Medical Conditions

Medication Tracker

Medication

Purpose

Dosage   **Dose & Time**

Start Date   **Stop Date**

Side effects / notes   ....

....

Medication

Purpose

Dosage   **Dose & Time**

Start Date   **Stop Date**

Side effects / notes   ....

....

Notes

Blood Sugar Tracker

Week: **Date:**

Sun		Mon		Tue		Wed		Thu		Fri		Sat		
B	A	B	A	B	A	B	A	B	A	B	A	B	A	
														1
														2
														3
														4

Week :   **Date :**

Sun		Mon		Tue		Wed		Thu		Fri		Sat		
B	A	B	A	B	A	B	A	B	A	B	A	B	A	
														1
														2
														3
														4

Note:

- B = Before
- A = After

Our Fitness Goals

START DATE	END DATE

SIZING	GOAL	START	END
Weight			
BMI			
Chest			
Arms			
Waist			
Hips			
Thighs			
Calves			

OUR MOTIVATION TO STAY FIT

HABITS TO START/STOP

Workout Log

Date: _____ / _____ / _____   Total Workout Time: _____

EXERCISE	Set 1		Set 2	
	Weight	Reps	Weight	Reps

NOTES

THE

POWER OF 2:

WORK+DESIRE=SUCCESS

Soul

|

*How to care for the spiritual health of the
business and marital relationship*

#THEPOWEROF2X

Prayer Strategy

"Therefore a man shall leave his father and mother and be joined to his wife, and they shall become one flesh."

- Genesis 2:24 [NKJV] -

"Let all that you do be done with love."

- 1 Corinthians 16:14 [NKJV] -

"So then, they are no longer two but one flesh. Therefore what God has joined together, let not man separate."

- Matthew 19:6 [NKJV] -

"Be anxious for nothing, but in everything by prayer and supplication, with thanksgiving, let your requests be made known to God; and the peace of God, which surpasses all understanding, will guard your hearts and minds through Christ Jesus."

- Philippians 4:6-7 [NKJV] -

"Though one may be overpowered by another, two can withstand him. And a threefold cord is not quickly broken."

- ECCLESIASTES 4:12 [NKJV] -

Now, your turn! Together, research Biblical scriptures and principles for marriage God's Way. This is the fun part :)

Prayer Strategy

FOR COUPLES

Prayer Strategy
FOR COUPLES

Prayer Strategy

CREATIVE WORKSHOP

THE
POWER OF 2:
WORK+DESIRE=SUCCESS

Money

How to care for the mental health of the
business and marital relationship

#THEPOWEROF2X

Financial Goal

OUR WHY

OUR MONEY GOAL:

STARTING BALANCE:

REQUIRED NUMBER & ACTION
TO REACH MONEY GOAL:

Per
DAY: _____

Per
MONTH: _____

DUE DATE:

NOTES

www.thepowerof2x.com

Savings Goal

GOAL:	DATE	AMOUNT

SAVINGS ACCOUNT #:

DEADLINE:

TOTAL:

Monthly Expenses

Essential Expenses (60%)

HOUSING

Mortgage/Rent $ _____

Home Maintenance $ _____

Renters' Insurance $ _____

Utilities (Gas, Water, Electric etc. $ _____

_____ $ _____

HEALTH CARE/INSURANCE

Health Ins. $ _____

Life Insurance $ _____

Disability Income Insurance $ _____

Long Term Care Ins. $ _____

$ _____

Saving/Investing (20%)

Emergency Fund $ _____

College Fund $ _____

Retirement Saving (401k, Roth IRA) $ _____

Regular Savings $ _____

_____ $ _____

HOUSEHOLD/PERSONAL

Groceries $ _____

Personal Care $ _____

Laundry/Dry Clean $ _____

Professional Dues $ _____

_____ $ _____

_____ $ _____

TRANSPORTATION

Auto Payments $ _____

Gas $ _____

Maintenance/ License $ _____

Parking/Tolls $ _____

Auto Insurance $ _____

_____ $ _____

Discretionary Expenses (20%)

Cable/Phone/Internet $ _____

Dining Out $ _____

Movies/Events/Hobbies $ _____

Vacation $ _____

Gifts/Charity $ _____

Credit Card Debt Repayment $ _____

_____ $ _____

_____ $ _____

_____ $ _____

CHILDREN

Childcare $ _____

Education $ _____

Allowances $ _____

_____ $ _____

_____ $ _____

STUDENT LOANS

Loan 1 $ _____

Loan 2 $ _____

Loan 3 $ _____

Loan 4 $ _____

Subtotal $ _____

Net Income $ _____

(Total Expenses) $ _____

Surplus/(Deficit) $ _____

Budget Notes

★ ★ ★

part two

THE POWER OF 2

BUILD YOUR BUSINESS

Date: _____   Partners: _____

Goals Planner
FOR THE BUSINESS

Our Goals	Motivations

Actions to Take	Deadline
☐ _____	_____
☐ _____	_____
☐ _____	_____
☐ _____	_____
☐ _____	_____
☐ _____	_____

Important Dates

January
- ○ _____
- ○ _____
- ○ _____

February
- ○ _____
- ○ _____
- ○ _____

March
- ○ _____
- ○ _____
- ○ _____

April
- ○ _____
- ○ _____
- ○ _____

May
- ○ _____
- ○ _____
- ○ _____

June
- ○ _____
- ○ _____
- ○ _____

July
- ○ _____
- ○ _____
- ○ _____

August
- ○ _____
- ○ _____
- ○ _____

September
- ○ _____
- ○ _____
- ○ _____

October
- ○ _____
- ○ _____
- ○ _____

November
- ○ _____
- ○ _____
- ○ _____

December
- ○ _____
- ○ _____
- ○ _____

Note :
_____
_____

Weekly Planner

URGENT

- ○ ....
- ○ ....
- ○ ....

sunday

- ○ ....
- ○ ....
- ○ ....

monday

- ○ ....
- ○ ....
- ○ ....

tuesday

- ○ ....
- ○ ....
- ○ ....

wednesday

- ○ ....
- ○ ....
- ○ ....

thursday

- ○ ....
- ○ ....
- ○ ....

friday

- ○ ....
- ○ ....
- ○ ....

saturday

- ○ ....
- ○ ....
- ○ ....

CREATIVE
WORKSHOP

THE

POWER OF 2:

WORK+DESIRE=SUCCESS

Brainstorm Business Ideas

How To Succeed in Business and in Marriage

#THEPOWEROF2X

Business Brainstorm

What are our skills, gifts, strengths? How can this translate into a business?

What problem are we trying to solve?

Who is our ideal customer?

What will give us a competitive advantage so we stand out from everyone else?

Business Overview

S M T W T F S

Date:

Business Structure:

Business Name:

Tagline:

Website:

Products & Services	Mission Statement
_____	_____
_____	_____
_____	_____
_____	_____
_____	_____

Social Media Handles:

Avatar/Ideal Client Name:

Target Market

Date:

Up Close and Personal with Our Target Market:

Who do we serve?

Who is our ideal client?

What is their income level?

What is their motivation?

What is their problem or fear?

Solutions to their problem (our products/services):

Competition Tracker

COMPETITOR -

COMPETITOR EDGE -

WEBSITE -

COMPETITOR -

COMPETITOR EDGE -

WEBSITE -

COMPETITOR -

COMPETITOR EDGE -

WEBSITE -

ANALYSIS

NOTES

Date: _____ Day: _____

SWOT Analysis

Strengths	Weaknesses

Opportunities	Threats

NOTES

NOTES

THE

POWER OF 2:

WORK+DESIRE=SUCCESS

Starting a Business Checklist

Creating a filing system to keep the business organized and running like a well-oiled machine

#THEPOWEROF2X

Business-in-a-Glance

This page keeps all of your business paperwork and information in one place. Once you begin to invest in your technology, team, marketing, coaching and professional development, you will definitely need a one-stop shop to track this information. Hint: You can also use this for onboarding new staff!

BUSINESS NAME	**BUSINESS EMAIL**
BUSINESS WEBSITE	**BUSINESS PHONE #**
BUSINESS ADDRESS	**BUSINESS BANK ACCOUNT #**
STATE ANNUAL REGISTRATION DATE	**DUNS #**
	EIN #

Payment Gateway(s) - the more ways people can pay you, the more ways you can get paid! Start an account with as many of these as possible in the business name.

- PayPal
- Stripe
- Moonclerk
- CashApp
- Zelle
- Authorize.net
- WooCommerce
- Shopify
- Square

Date: _____   Day: _____

To Do List

To Do List	S	M	T	W	T	F	S
	☐	☐	☐	☐	☐	☐	☐
	☐	☐	☐	☐	☐	☐	☐
	☐	☐	☐	☐	☐	☐	☐
	☐	☐	☐	☐	☐	☐	☐
	☐	☐	☐	☐	☐	☐	☐
	☐	☐	☐	☐	☐	☐	☐
	☐	☐	☐	☐	☐	☐	☐
	☐	☐	☐	☐	☐	☐	☐
	☐	☐	☐	☐	☐	☐	☐
	☐	☐	☐	☐	☐	☐	☐
	☐	☐	☐	☐	☐	☐	☐

NOTES

NOTES

THE

POWER OF 2:

WORK + DESIRE = SUCCESS

Business Profit Plan

How To Succeed in Business and in Marriage

#THEPOWEROF2X

Budget Plan

TOTAL EXPENSE:

TOTAL INCOME:

TOTAL SAVING:

INCOME

DATE	AMOUNT

FIXED EXPENSES

DATE	AMOUNT

OTHER EXPENSES

DATE	AMOUNT

Bill Checklist

MONTHLY	AMOUNT	DUE	✓
			●
			○
			●
			○
			●
			○
			●
			○

ANUALLY	AMOUNT	DUE	✓
			●
			●
			●
			●
			●

Expense Tracker

MONTH:

DATE	ITEM	SPENT	REMAINS

Debt Tracker

Min. Payment:

Total Payment:

MONTH	AMOUNT	BILL

NOTES

NOTES

CREATIVE WORKSHOP

THE

POWER OF 2:

WORK+DESIRE=SUCCESS

Digital Marketing Strategy

How To Succeed in Business and in Marriage

#THEPOWEROF2X

Marketing Plan

What is our brand strategy? How do we want to appear to the world?

What is our product or service line?

Will we have a referral affiliate or ambassador program? If so, who will manage it?

How do we track the results and how often?

Resource: To get media exposure for your new business (press releases and all), register an account with Haro (Help A Reporter Out) at https://app.helpareporter.com, then submit pitches to be featured in the media.

Find out more about HARO and how to use the database: https://www.brigittelyons.com/haro/

Marketing Plan

S M T W T F S

Date:

Channel	Marketing Tactics	One-time Cost	Monthly Cost
Total Cost			

Social Media Audit

Current Platforms Used:

Know Your Numbers:

Like	Share	Comments	Views

Best Time(s) to Post

Notes

Engagement Analysis: What Works vs What Doesn't

Social Media Stats

Platform				

Month	Week 1	Week 2	Week 3	Week 4
Jan				
Feb				
Mar				
Apr				
May				
Jun				
Jul				
Aug				
Sep				
Oct				
Nov				
Dec				

Notes/Trends/Recommendations:

Content Creator

Main Topic Posts

_____

_____

_____

Frequency

☐ Daily

☐ Weekly

☐ Monthly

☐ _____

Specific Posts

_____

_____

_____

Frequency

☐ Daily

☐ Weekly

☐ Monthly

☐ _____

Famous Quotes

Links to Social Media Platforms

MONTHLY PLANNER

IDENTIFY HOLIDAYS, SPECIAL OCCASIONS, ETC.

SUN	MON	TUE	WED	THU	FRI	SAT

WEEKLY GOALS:

Write goals to match holidays and special occasions. Your marketing strategy is based on what is happening in the world. A little research is required here.

Letter to My Partner

Date: Month: Year:

Letter to My Partner

Date: Month: Year:

NOTES

NOTES

CREATIVE WORKSHOP

THE
POWER OF 2:
WORK+DESIRE=SUCCESS

Resources

How To Succeed in Business and in Marriage

#THEPOWEROF2X

Resources

HIRING STAFF

www.fiverr.com
www.guru.com
www.upwork.com
www.internships.com
www.indeed.com

ONLINE REGISTRATION

BUSINESS REGISTRATION

Register business with your state › Google "How to register business in ...Name of State..."

CONFERENCE CALL SERVICES

- Zoom (most popular)
- Google Meet
- Free Conference Call
- Free Conferencing
- Uber Conference

EMAIL MARKETING

www.ontraport.com
www.mailerlite.com
www.mailchimp.com
www.aweber.com
www.getresponse.com

COACHING

Eric Kirk
Life & Business Coach

www.thepowerof2x.com

SCHEDULING TOOLS

www.calendly.com
www.acuity.com
www.vCita.com

PURCHASE WEBSITE DOMAIN

https://iwantmyname.com

PROJECT MANAGMENT TOOLS

www.trello.com
www.monday.com
www.asana.com

Hello, I'm Eric Kirk

Author, The Power of 2

Eric Kirk, a native of Bessemer, Alabama, is a life coach, motivational speaker, author, and entrepreneur.

He founded Kirk Enterprises, where he is currently the CEO and the Co-Founder of Brother to Brother, a men's empowerment group.

Eric believes that every individual has greatness inside of them, and all anyone needs is help.

Follow Eric on Social Media:
Facebook & Twitter: Eric Kirk
Instagram: Eric Kirk_The potentialProtector

www.thepowerof2x.com

Other Works by the Author

Eric Kirk

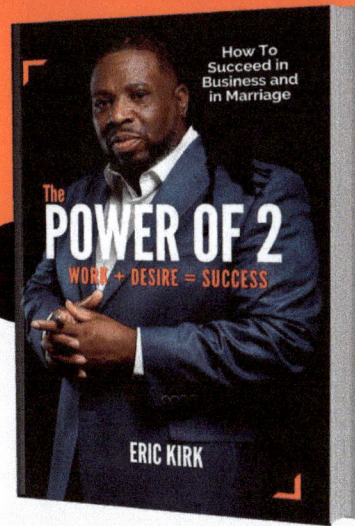

The Power of 2 illustrates how biblical wisdom helps solve daily problems– from how to keep work issues from spilling over into the home front, to understanding what makes men think the way they do. Both spouses needs often times are different and at times may be contrary, yet this book reveals how both people can get all their needs met without sacrificing one another's individual desire. It is The Power of 2 simplified.

The main characters of The Power of 2, Werk and Desire, learn how to navigate their new lives together, facing some of the same challenges most marriages face today, at the time this book was written.

This book covers four main points:

1. You must have a firm foundation of biblical principles in order to be successful;
2. You must act on your principles from the start, whether in business or marriage;
3. You'll still experience some tough times; and
4. You can (and will) succeed with God's help!

www.thepowerof2x.com

THE
POWER OF 2:

WORK+DESIRE=SUCCESS

W O R K B O O K *for couples*

How To Succeed in
Business and in Marriage

www.ingramcontent.com/pod-product-compliance
Lightning Source LLC
Chambersburg PA
CBHW061412090426

42741CB00023B/3489